*Practical Faith Principles*

# PASSING IT ON
## *Practical Faith Principles*

*by* BETTY BATTS

# AMBASSADOR INTERNATIONAL
GREENVILLE, SOUTH CAROLINA & BELFAST, NORTHERN IRELAND

www.ambassador-international.com

# PASSING IT ON
*Practical Faith Principles*

© 2011 Betty Batts
All rights reserved

Printed in the United States of America

ISBN: 978-1-935507-43-7

Unless otherwise stated, all Scripture quotations are from THE HOLY BIBLE, NEW INTERNATIONAL VERSION®, NIV® Copyright © 1973, 1978, 1984, 2010 by Biblica, Inc.™ Used by permission. All rights reserved worldwide.

Cover Design & Page Layout by David Siglin of A&E Media

AMBASSADOR INTERNATIONAL
Emerald House
427 Wade Hampton Blvd.
Greenville, SC 29609, USA
www.ambassador-international.com

AMBASSADOR BOOKS
The Mount
2 Woodstock Link
Belfast, BT6 8DD, Northern Ireland, UK
www.ambassador-international.com

*The colophon is a trademark of Ambassador*

Patti M. Hummel
President & Agent
THE BENCHMARK GROUP LLC, Nashville, TN
*www.benchmarkgrouppublishers.com*

This book was edited by:
Vicki Huffman, VP/Senior Editor
THE BENCHMARK GROUP LLC, NASHVILLE, TN
*benchmarkgroup2@aol.com*

## Introduction

Younger generations are notoriously bad at listening. Which is a most ironic trait. What we most need—wisdom—we're too impatient to seek. I suppose this is why the father in Proverbs incessantly reminds his son: "Hey! Would you listen for a moment?" We're busy and arrogant. We rarely stop to consider the impact our decisions will have on the future. Rare are the moments we stop to ask directions from people who've already been down the road we're traveling. As far as we're concerned, we've got this. Our pride keeps us from asking, and our ambition keeps us from admitting we *should* ask. And so we set off, repeating mistakes which could have easily been avoided—had we listened.

We all make mistakes. Eventually, we reach a place where we can admit them. *("If I knew then what I know now, life would have been much less painful.")* For some odd reason, we learn best the hard way. Mistakes are our most effective tutors. This is why someone described pain as the megaphone God uses to get our attention. Undoubtedly, there are numerous self-inflicted wounds we could avoid if we would seek the counsel of those who experienced them firsthand–if we would listen to the wisdom around us.

I once asked a "saintly" patriarch in our church an important question: "If you could do one thing differently in your life, what would it be?" I expected a really dramatic answer, something akin to a slogan you might find at the bottom of an inspirational poster. What I heard was neither dramatic or cliché. It was elementary and wise: "I'd pray more often and start praying sooner." Translation? I'd be less dependent on my own strength and wisdom and more dependent on God's. In other words, "I'd ask for help more often than I did." If a man who had the perspective of seventy years behind him admitted this need, what does that say about my need–and yours?

*Passing it On: Practical Principles for Life* by Betty Batts is a treasure of hard-earned and keenly insightful wisdom on everything from prayer to organization. The variety of topics reflects the life Betty has enjoyed. It's been full. She hasn't wasted any experience—good or bad. Betty has taken copious notes about these life experiences, seeking to reduce them to easily transferable principles. This book is a gift to our overloaded and overconfident generation. The reader will be thankful she has seen fit to pass her wisdom on.

Rather than coming across like a stale speech or canned platitudes, her assemblage of wisdom is like having a conversation with a trusted friend and mentor. Through humor, poetry, irony, parable and firsthand accounts, she urges the reader to make the most of life's experiences. Her wisdom is obvious, her sincerity undeniable. As a personal friend of Betty and one who has benefited from her encouragement, I can tell you that she lives what she believes. Everything she writes has been lived first. There are probably things Betty wishes she had done differently, or better, but there is no experience she has wasted.

—BYRON YAWN, *Senior Pastor*
*Community Bible Church*
*Nashville, TN*

# Table of Contents

**Trust: 13-16**
*Defined and Portrayed*

**Grace: 17-20**
*Given and Received*

**Prayer: 21-24**
*Asking Rightly*

**Servanthood: 25-28**
*Duties and Provisions*

**Friendship: 29-31**
*What Friendship Is*

**Pastor's Wife: 32-34**
*Reflections Past and Present*

**Money: 35-38**
*Pitfalls and Purposes*

**Work Ethic: 39-42**
*The Ethics of Hard Work*

**Our Words: 43-45**
*Helping or Hurting*

**Change: 46-48**
*Spiritual Change or Foolish Changes*

**Joys of Hospitality: 49-52**
*Open Hearts = Open Homes*

**Being A Real Man: 53-58**
*Like Daniel*

**Finding A Husband: 59-61**
*And a Tribute to Mine*

**Engagements: 62-64**
*Ins and Outs*

**Love And Marriage: 65-71**
*Glowing and Growing*

**Wives: 72-75**
*Wise and Foolish*

**Mother: 76-79**
*To (P)raise a Child*

**Mother-in-Laws: 80-82**
*How Not to Be a Joke*

**Daughter-in-Law: 83-84**
*What Ruth Learned*

**Grandmother: 85-88**
*Memory Making*

**Valentine's Day: 89-92**
*Roses Say "I love you"*

**Clutter: 93-96**
*Here Today...More Tomorrow*

**Lessons From Animals: 97-101**
*Listen to the Animals*

**Growing Older: 102-105**
*My Grandmother Lee Ann Curtis*

**Ending Well: 106-109**
*My Grandfather Robert Belle Hearn*

# Trust

To put faith in
To depend on completely
To believe in totally
To commit yourself wholly.

TRUST leaves no room for fear
… for worry
… for doubt
… for anxiety.

GOD can be trusted completely
HE is trustworthy
HE knows you
HE loves you
HE has a plan for your life.

TRUST involves faith
when you don't understand
when the way is dark.

TRUST involves obedience
when you really trust
you will obey.

The better you get to know GOD
the easier it is to TRUST HIM.

Spend your life getting to know GOD
and TRUST will follow.

## A Story About Trust

My heart was pounding as I left the doctor's office after having heard a diagnosis I did not expect. I had come for a routine checkup, but my doctor began the exam by asking me if anyone in my family had Parkinson's Disease. I answered no, puzzled as to why he would bring it up. After my check-up, when I sat in his office he said I had the disease.

As I drove to the restaurant where I was to meet a friend for lunch, I pondered his words. BETTY, YOU HAVE PARKINSON'S DISEASE! The first thought that came into my mind was what Job had said so many years ago:

"Shall we receive good from the hands of God and not bad? The Lord gives and the Lord takes away. Blessed be the name of the Lord."

At that moment, I began to learn in a new way what it means to TRUST GOD.

It means to accept the truth that God knows what is best for me. It means to accept the fact that His will is not always what I would choose. It means that I am to trust God for strength for each day and not worry about the future.

As I reached the restaurant, I had a peace and calmness that enabled me to enjoy a lovely lunch and not to mention Parkinson's Disease.

# Grace

Limitless   Boundless   Matchless
All of God   Nothing of Us

Can Not Earn It   Do Not Deserve It
Salvation   By Grace Alone
Christian Living   By Grace Alone

All That I Am   All That I Do
All That I Have   All That I Know
Because of God's Grace

We Deserve Nothing   God Gives Us Everything
We Have No Power   God Gives Us His Power
We Have No Strength   God Give Us His Strength

We Are Weak   He Is Strong
We Are Nothing   He Is Everything
We Are Needy   He Is Rich

**GRACE** = **GOD**'S **R**ICHES
**A**T **C**HRIST'S **E**XPENSE

When We Understand Grace, We Have No Room for
Pride or a Judgmental Attitude

Serving God Earns No Merit
In Our Own Strength, We Are Failures
Only By Grace – Thru God's Power
Can We Serve Him

## A Story About Grace

While driving my granddaughter to her piano lesson, it became evident that we would be late. We had dawdled as we prepared to leave, and now we were suffering the consequences. Beth Ann became very upset and began to prod me to go faster and faster.

Against my better judgment I complied only to hear, almost immediately, a siren blaring from an approaching police car. I knew he was after me. As expected, he flashed his lights signaling me to pull over. As he approached my car, a sick feeling came over me. I realized I was guilty, no question about it. When he came to my car I spoke with a trembling, quiet voice: "I was speeding, I know, and I have no excuse. I am very sorry."

"This is a work zone, and it is very dangerous to speed thru this area. I am not going to give you a ticket. This is a warning. Remember to be more careful from now on." That was the unbelievable response of the officer.

I was amazed and answered, "This is grace. You didn't give me what I deserved but gave me what I did not deserve."

What a lesson of grace I learned that day. *God's grace.* We all deserve the punishment of death for our sins. But God in His grace took our punishment and allowed His Son to be put to death for all our sins.

Everything we have is undeserved and given to us by God our Father who promises to give us richly all things to enjoy.

# Prayer

Don't tell God what He should do.

Ask God what you should do.

Demanding things from God is like saying

"We know better than God."

"Thy will be done" should be the underlying attitude in all our prayers.

Asking is admitting our needs.

Asking is accepting His answer.

Asking reveals dependence on and trust in God.

The basic lesson we must learn is that we can trust God.

When we trust God the worry is gone.

He knows what is best for us.

"Pray without ceasing."

I Thessalonians 5:17

"In everything give thanks."

I Thessalonians 5:18

"Delight yourself in the Lord and He will give you the desires of your heart."

Psalm 37:4

## A Story About Prayer

I was just finishing my shower when the phone rang. I found out I needed to get to the hospital to see a friend whose husband was recovering from a heart attack. I was concerned because I knew he was supposed to go home that day. It appeared that something had gone wrong. The hair dryer seemed to be working slowly as I hurried to get ready to go to the hospital.

Finally I was on my way. As I drove I began to pray, "Lord, you can't let him die. He has three children and one is nine months old."

The Lord seemed to answer clearly (although not audibly), "You cannot tell Me what I can or cannot do."

I then prayed, "Lord, please don't let him die until Jerry gets back from Portland." (My husband was there at a convention.)

The Lord seemed to answer again, "You cannot tell Me what I can or cannot do."

A third time I prayed, "Lord, please don't let him die until I get there. His wife should not have to be alone at this time."

Again the Lord seemed to answer, "You cannot tell Me what I can or cannot do." It finally hit me.

I then prayed, "Lord, may Your will be done. Give us the strength to get through this day."

He answered, "Yes, my child, I will."

And He did.

# On Being A Servant

**A SERVANT**

Belongs to his master

Obeys his master

Does his master's will

Has no will of his own

Puts his master before himself

**GOD IS MY MASTER**

We do His will

We belong to Christ

We obey His Word

### A Servant Does Not Say:

Anything but that

When I am not busy

Let someone else do it

I need more time to think about it

Those people do not appreciate me

### A Servant Says:

Not my will but yours be done

I am serving the Lord not people

My desire is to please God not people

People disappoint us – God never does

### Man's Perspective:

If you want to be great, put yourself first (no one else will).

### God's Perspective:

If you want to be great, be a servant.

## A Story About Serving the Lord

The Miracle Piano

Many years ago my husband was pastor of a small church in the capitol of Alabama, Montgomery. The boys were growing up and in the process we insisted that they at least try to learn to play the piano. Our older son Mark gave up after a year, but Larry was more interested and continued to take lessons. We had a very old, out-of-tune piano which had been put in the parsonage by one of the members who wanted to dispose of it. One day after practicing on it, Larry announced that he would not take any more lessons unless he had a better piano on which to practice.

Jerry and I discussed the problem. My solution was to buy a better piano with the raise in pay we felt we would receive in the coming year. The night the budget for the coming year was discussed, I could hardly wait for Jerry to come home from the board meeting. But, to my amazement, Jerry was only to receive a pittance of a raise.

I could not believe it. How could we buy a piano? Didn't God care? Didn't the board care? I struggled with feelings of self-pity, anger and resentment all weekend. On Monday morning, the phone rang. It was a friend in the church. Her first words were, "Betty, I want you to go to a piano store and pick out any brand new piano you want, and I will buy it for you."

I learned an invaluable lesson that day. We serve God, not people. When we have a need, we should look to God to provide, not people. When He provides, He does it His way which is always better than man's way!

### The Rest of the Story

The husband of the lady who offered me the piano had recently died. After she received his insurance, she decided to give a portion of it to us for a new piano: our miracle piano.

# Friendship

QUALITIES OF BIBLICAL FRIENDSHIP

Commitment

John 15:12-15

Forgiveness

I Peter 4:8

Acceptance

Proverbs 27:6

Freedom

I Corinthians 13:4-8

EXAMPLES OF BIBLICAL FRIENDSHIP

David and Jonathan (I Samuel 18:1-3, 23:16-18)

Ruth and Naomi (Ruth 1:16-18, 3:1, 4:15)

## Principles of Friendship
## Learned from Experience

Friendship can be as strong as iron and as fragile as a rose

Friendship cannot be exclusive – it has to be free

True friendship does not have conditions or expectations

To be a friend to only one person is not love but possessiveness

Friendship can be very deep – but that takes time and shared experiences

### Love is not Shallow – Love Deeply
### Love is not Selfish – Love Widely
### Love is not Possessive – Love Freely
### Love is not Perfect – Love Forgivingly

"Two are better than one, because they have a good reward for their work:
If one falls down, his friend can help him up:
But pity the man who falls and has no one to help him up!" Ecclesiastes 4:9-10

## The Colors of Friendship

*Yellow is the sunshine we share with all our friends*
*Lots of friends are with us when everything is fine.*
*Blue is how we sometimes feel and then we need a friend*
*Who understands and listens and helps to make us mend*
*We think of green and know that green and growth go hand in hand*
*Friendships must grow and, if they don't, they end.*

*A few friends are like rainbows with their glistening hue*
*Thru good and bad, thru joy and pain*
*Even then, they are there for you*
*The secret of enjoying all these precious friends*
*Is to be a friend yourself and reach out to all you can.*

# On Being A Pastor's Wife

### Principles Learned Through the Years:

Look for the good in people – not for the bad

Serve your people – don't wait for them to serve you

Pray for them – more than you pray for yourself

### Being "On Display"

Be what God wants you to be – not what people want you to be

Be yourself – not what others expect you to be

Be a model of stronger/weaker brother relationships

### Priorities

Keep priorities in line with God's standard

God first

Husband and family second

Ministry third

### Being A Servant

Remember you are only a servant – a servant of God

A servant has no rights of his own

His only desire is to serve the master

### On the Tongue

It can be a curse or a blessing

Keep husband's confidences

"A soft answer turns away wrath"

Listen more – talk less

### On Children

Give them unconditional love – make sure they are secure

Never let them feel that the ministry is more important than them

Help them see what a privilege it is to be a pastor's child

*Dedicated to the four congregations that we have served for over fifty years: I learned from each one and was greatly loved by each one. I can only thank God for His grace.*

## My Pastor's Wife: Karon Walls

After being a pastor's wife for more than fifty years, it has been interesting serving in a church where my husband is not the senior pastor. My first meeting with my pastor's wife was lunch. I was anxious to get to know her and express my support for her and acceptance of her.

I was delighted to see that she felt comfortable just being herself. She did not feel the need to be a people pleaser, nor did she have a persecution complex and feel sorry for herself. I did sense that she had an intimate relationship with her Lord with a great desire to know His will for her life and her time.

As time has passed, we have become good friends and I continue to admire her dedicated life. I see and admire her love for her husband and children. I appreciate her servant spirit and her sensitivity to God's will for her life.

Karon Walls is a pastor's wife worthy of "double honor."

# On Money

Don't love it
Don't lose it
Don't waste it.

Spend it carefully
Give it sacrificially
Save it wisely.

Give generously to God
Give freely to others
Spend prudently on yourself.

"He who loves money never has enough."
"Money can take wings and fly away."
"The *love* of money is the root of all evil."
"God loves a cheerful giver."

Never spend more than you make.

"The borrower is slave to the lender."

Always give to God first.

You can never out-give God.

(*Principles from Proverbs, I Corinthians and I Timothy*)

"He is no fool who gives what he cannot keep to gain what he cannot lose."

~Jim Elliot

## Stories About Money

When Jerry and I married, he was in seminary and I was still in college. Our finances were very limited to say the least. Jerry was working evenings earning one dollar and ten cents an hour. He was paid weekly and beginning with his first pay check, we gave the Lord three dollars and thirty three cents per week.

I know that God did not need that little bit of money but we needed to give it to learn that where your treasure is there will your heart be also. Because of our limited means, it was probably harder to give that little bit of money than it was later on when we made more money. But we learned a lesson we have never forgotten. If you really love God, you will give Him your best, even if it is a great sacrifice.

We have always been softies when people are in need and ask for help. Every time we resolve to be tough and not be taken in by some scam, someone comes along with a really good story. We have decided that we would rather err on the side of helping someone who really did not need help than to take a chance on not helping someone who really did.

When I had to go through some of Jerry's father's business papers, I found a personal loan agreement for $15,000. Years before, his father had loaned the money to a friend who was having a hard time financially. The sad thing about the agreement was that his friend had never paid the money back. God had blessed and prospered Jerry's father so much. I have to believe it was because when he saw his brother in need he was willing to help him in a tangible way. He didn't love money, but he used his money to serve others.

I want to have that same attitude about money.

# On Work

*What is your work ethic?*
*How does it compare to the biblical standard?*

### BIBLICAL STANDARD

Ecclesiastes 5:18-20 – Satisfaction in your work

Happy in your work

Work a gift from God

Colossians 3:17 – Whatever you do, do in Jesus Christ's name

Give thanks to God

Colossians 3:23 – Whatever you do, work at it with all your heart

Working for the Lord, not men

### SLUGGARD

Proverbs 20:13 – loving sleep will make one poor

Proverbs 24:30-34 – laziness brings on poverty

Proverbs 12:24 – laziness ends in slave labor

## Hard Worker

Proverbs 30:24-25 – learn hard work from the ant

Proverbs 28:19 – don't chase fantasies

Proverbs 22:29 – be skilled in your work

## A Good Work Ethic

Our son was the janitor at our church when he was a young teen. His father had taught him very carefully and thoroughly how to do the work in the best way. The floors in the educational building were vinyl tile and had gotten very scuffed and needed attention badly. Mark and his buddy offered to strip and wax all the floors during spring break. His father felt it was a big job and warned him about how long it might take. But nothing would deter them and on Monday morning, bright and early, the project was begun.

As expected, the job was bigger than they had thought and as the week wore on it became apparent that it would take the whole week to complete. As they neared the end of the job, their thoughts turned to money. How much would they receive for the work? They were paid by the day and therefore they thought they might be paid that amount for each of the days they had worked. But that was not the case. When they received their pay check, there was only one extra day of pay for the whole job. Mark was furious (as were his parents).

His father very wisely gave him three avenues of recourse. He could complain to the deacon board. He could quit the job in protest and develop a bitter grudge toward the men who made the decision. He could learn from the experience the things he needed to learn: He should not take a job without knowing what the pay would be. He should count the cost before starting a job and be realistic about how much time it would take to complete.

Our son chose the latter recourse and continued to have a realistic work ethic throughout his days at that job. As he became an adult and worked for public companies, he had learned how to do his very best at whatever job he was given.

Ecclesiastes 9:10 "Whatever your hand finds to do, do it with all your might..."

# Our Words

THE WORDS WE SPEAK SHOULD BE:

TRUE – "A truthful witness does not deceive"

KIND – "A kind word cheers him up"

HOLY – "The mouth of the righteous is a fountain of life"

GUARDED – "He who guards his lips guards his life"

GENTLE – "A gentle answer turns away wrath"

HEALING – "The tongue that brings healing is a tree of life"

APT – "A man finds joy in giving an apt answer"

PLEASANT – "Pleasant words promote instruction"

PATIENT – "A patient man calms a quarrel"

RESTRAINED – "A man of knowledge uses words with restraint"

WISE – "The mouth of the righteous brings forth wisdom"

Our Words Should Not BE:

MALICIOUS – "A malicious man disguises himself with his lips"

QUARRELSOME – "A quarrelsome wife is like a constant dripping"

GOSSIPING – "The words of a man are like choice morsels"

RASH – "It is to a man's honor to avoid strife, but every fool is quick to quarrel"

*(These verses are all from the book of Proverbs.)*

## Hurtful Words

My younger sister's Sunday school class was having a party at our church. It was on a Saturday and, because my parents had to work, my mother asked me to ride the bus with my sister to the party. When we arrived at the church, her teacher with a puzzled look on her face asked why I had come. Before I could say a word she blurted out, "This party is for your sister's class not yours. We can't have children from other classes attending."

Crushed and humiliated, I disappeared in tears to the dark balcony above the auditorium. When the teacher found me, she probably expressed some words of apology and concern, but I don't remember them. I only remember the hurtful words that came from the teacher's lips.

# On Change

Change is all around us

God exemplified change in creation

when He made the Seasons

Day and night

Rain, snow, hail, tornados, hurricanes

The cycle of life

### Change Is Involved In Salvation

"If any man be in Christ he is a new creature,

old things are passed away all things are become new."

II Corinthians 5:17 KJV

Each person must change and become like a little child

to become a Christian.

### Growing In Christ Involves Change

"We are all being changed to be more like Christ."

All Growing Things change

Change involves risk

It is easier to stay the same, not to risk change

Do not be afraid to change.

"We shall all be changed."

God's message never changes.

God's methods do change.

**"DO NOT SAY OLD WAYS WERE BETTER."**

## Foolish Changes

When I was a young child, my father owned a small neighborhood grocery store. My mother also worked at the store, and I remember spending time with her there playing dominoes. I must have been only five or six years old. I remember that I didn't like always losing, so I put a small mark on the double five and the 6-4. After that I won almost all the time. My mother never could figure out why I won so much.

Even though I was winning, I found that suddenly all the joy of playing the game was gone. I tried to get the marks off the dominoes, but they would not come off. I found out that it was no fun to win when you don't do so honestly.

# Joys of Hospitality

## Commanded In Scripture

"Keep on loving each other as brothers. Do not forget to entertain strangers, for by so doing some people have entertained angels without knowing it." Hebrews 13:1-2

"Share with God's people who are in need. Practice hospitality." Romans 12:13

"Practice hospitality without grumbling." I Peter 4:9

## Enjoyed By Jesus

The wedding at Cana of Galilee – John 2

*Modeled importance of marriage reception*

Dinner at the taxpayer's house – Mark 2

*Willing to associate with sinners*

Dinner with Mary and Martha – John 12

*Pointed out guests are more important than food*

The last supper with His disciples – John 13
*Fellowshipped with friends over a meal*

### Exemplified By The Shunammite Woman
A generous heart – II Kings 4
Unselfish with her means
Concerned and thoughtful about her guest
Attentive to details

### Hospitality vs. Entertaining
Hospitality – sharing because we care about others
Entertaining – to impress, expect return of favor
Hospitality – putting love in action, unselfishness

## Real Hospitality

Tucked away in the book of Second Kings there is a delightful story about a woman who showed real hospitality. The Bible says that she was a prominent woman, but her concern was not to entertain prominent people. Her concern was for the man of God. Each time the prophet traveled by her house, the woman would persuade Elisha to eat dinner with her. This became their regular routine. After some time, the woman had an idea. She excitedly told her husband, he consented and soon the project was done. They had built a room on to their house and furnished it with everything the prophet would need to spend the night: a bed, table, chair, even a lamp stand. It was obvious that the room was made and furnished with loving, thoughtful hands. Every time Elijah traveled in the direction of the woman's house, he spent the night in his special room.

What a wonderful story of hospitality. The woman was only concerned about Elisha's needs and doing everything she could to meet those needs. She was not thinking of herself or impressing others. That is real hospitality.

It is not surprising that in our modern homes the smallest rooms are often the dining room and the guest bedroom. That says a lot about where our priorities are. But the book of Proverbs offers those who practice hospitality this promise, "A generous man will prosper; he who refreshes others will himself be refreshed" (Proverbs 11:25).

# On Being A Real Man

### BE CAREFUL OF YOUR WALK WITH GOD
"Man, what does the Lord require of you?
To act justly and to love mercy
and to walk humbly with your God."

### BE CAREFUL OF YOUR WALK WITH OTHERS
"Speak for those who cannot speak for themselves
and all who are desolate.
Speak up and judge fairly.
Defend the rights of the poor and needy."

### BE CAREFUL ABOUT WOMEN
"Do not spend your strength on women,
especially those who ruin kings."

BE CAREFUL ABOUT STRONG DRINK

"It is not for rulers [*real men*] to drink wine

Or beer lest they drink and forget

What the law decrees."

Micah 5: 8;   Proverbs 31:1-3

*Dedicated to my four grandsons: Joshua Batts, David Batts, Jonah Lathbury and Ben Smolin*

# Daniel – A Real Man

Daniel is one man in the Bible who passed the test of living a godly life in a very ungodly world. He was admired by the godly people of his day as well as the ungodly. He was honored because of his godly life, but he was also persecuted because of it. Through it all, Daniel remained true to his God. He has gone down in history as a man who could be a success in public life without compromising his faith. What a challenge for people in public life today!

## True to His Convictions

When Daniel and his friends were taken to Babylon and put in the king's palace to be trained for public service, they were served food and drink that as Jews they were not to eat. Daniel, wisely and without pride, asked the official in charge if they could eat other food. He even said he would go back to the original food if the test showed they were being harmed.

### Knew Importance of Prayer

When the king wanted his dream interpreted and no one could, Daniel offered to pray for the answer. He asked his three friends to pray with him. When the king received his answer and wanted to praise Daniel, instead Daniel gave all the credit to God. When Daniel knew that if he prayed he would be thrown in the lion's den, he continued to pray with his windows open three times a day. It is said he thanked the Lord when he was praying. And God did deliver him!

### Humble Not Proud

Pride goes before a fall. Daniel warned King Nebuchadnezzar that God would punish him if he was proud. Daniel always had a humble spirit, even when he was in the lion's den.

### Competent, Dependable, Honest In His Work

When Daniel's enemies were trying to bring him down,

they admitted that they could find nothing wrong in how he did in his job. The only way they could charge him was by accusing him of something concerning his faith.

### Respected By Ungodly Leaders

Daniel served all his life in a Godless country. He was a foreigner, a Jew. And yet he rose to the third highest rank in the kingdom. And through it all he remained true to his God.

### A Man of Character

Lived in a foreign land
In training to be a leader
Stood by his convictions
Was gracious in his request for different food
Was willing to be put to the test

### A Man of Prayer

When crisis came Daniel asked for time to pray
Called his friends to join him in prayer
Gave God the credit for answer to his prayer

### A Man of Principle

Did his job with honesty, integrity, skill, loyalty

His enemies could not find any fault in his work

They could only accuse him because of his faith in God

### A Man of Faith

Prayed when he knew he could suffer

Thanked God even when things were dark

### An Example For Us All

# On Finding A Husband

### A Maiden's Prayer

Dear wise and loving God above,

Show me the man that I should love

May he be good and wise and true

May he have faith and believe in You

Grant him a smile for each tomorrow

May he have joy in pain and sorrow

Let him have faults dear Lord, You see

I don't want him too much better than me

But this above all else I ask

As I give unto You this task

First dear Lord he must love You

And then may he find that he loves me too.

—Author unknown

# On Being A Biblical Husband

A Tribute to My Husband

(Character traits from the book of Proverbs)

A generous man

"A generous man shall prosper"

A good man

"A righteous man leads a blameless life"

A man of knowledge

"A man of knowledge uses words with restraint"

A faithful man

"A faithful man will be richly blessed"

A man of integrity

"A man of integrity walks securely"

## Commitment

He walks with God

He loves his wife as Christ loved the church

He puts others before himself

He finds joy in serving others

## Evaluation

"If anyone wants to be great, let him be a servant"

# Getting Engaged

You need to be mature to make such important decisions
To become engaged cannot be a rash or hurried decision

GOD MUST DIRECT AND GUIDE THIS DECISION
Engagement is the formal beginning of a lifetime together

WORDS OF WISDOM FOR BEGINNING MARRIAGE
LISTEN – especially to your wife
Make that your lifetime habit
LEARN – from the mistakes of others
You can't live long enough to make them all yourself
LOVE – your wife as Christ loved the church
Make Him your model of sacrificial love
LIFETIME – this decision is for life
Forever – for always – and no matter what

# A Broken Engagement

They were in love – so much in love

The time was right – the end in sight

A ring was bought – and worn with pride

But deep inside his heart of hearts

A nagging thought that would not die

About his life that lay ahead

About his faith that seemed was gone

He knew that God should be the first

in all he did – in all he loved

He also knew the girl who had

his soul – his heart – his ring – his love

Did not even know his God at all

What could he do? What could he do?

The battle raged and would not cease

One day God spoke so loud and clear

He could not deny nor could he miss
What God had said — He had to choose
between the two he loved the most
His God or her
What could he do? He never could
but God gave strength to follow through
And when he did God blessed his life
And gave him one who loved his God
And put Him first in all she did.
We move ahead some forty years
And find that they are still in love
Both with their God and one another.
—A true story

## Undiminished Love

Charge given to Jonah and Beth Ann Lathbury by her grandfather, Jerry M. Batts, on the occasion of their wedding, January 28, 2006

There are several kinds of love:
- Selfish: I love you because of what you do for me.
- Sexual: I get gratification out of the relationship.
- Social: Enjoy being together, common interests
- Committed: Inner soul responses to each other
- Spiritual: God's love, the agape kind

### Personal – He loved us

God has pursued a relationship with you. He took the initiative to pursue you and bring you to Himself. If you had been left to your own plans, you would never have a relationship. Let your love for each other not wait or hold back from reaching out at any time, no matter what the case may be. God's love moved Him to communicate His heart to you. He is unreservedly open about His desires for you. He said, "I do not call you servants but friends because a servant does not know what his master is doing." Real friends are open and honest with each other. When you "speak the truth in love" with each other you will find resolutions for your differences. If you try to suppress them they will fester and poison your marriage.

### UNCONDITIONAL – NOT THAT WE LOVED GOD

There was nothing lovely about any of us when compared to the person of God. He has not loved you because of who you are but because He knew what you could become by the power of His transforming love. Neither has He loved you because of something you have done for Him. His love is perfectly unconditional toward you, and it always will be. When you are tempted to wait on the other to return love before you do, refresh your thoughts with this perfect pattern of love.

## Sacrificial – God sent His Son as an atoning sacrifice

For the giver of genuine love there is always a price to pay. No love is given without cost to the giver. Personal interests and desires cannot be placed before you have done your best to lay down your life for the other. Jonah, to love Beth Ann in this way will demonstrate to everyone the kind of sacrificial love the Lord Jesus has for all who are in His forever family.

## Beneficial – For our sins

Jesus' sacrificial love has bought great benefits to all who have received it. His love met your greatest need, which was to remove the otherwise insurmountable barrier between you and your Creator God. Your sin debt was far greater than you or anyone else could pay. In the pursuit of love for each other, ask God for wisdom to understand what the other's real needs are. That makes it imperative for you to continue to know each other more deeply each day. Intimacy has no substitute in the pursuit of God's kind of love.

## Motivational

"... if we love each other, God lives in us and His love is made complete in us ... We love him because He first loved us." (I John 4:12, 19)

You must constantly engage with God and His love as your first priority. It is only as your personal heart is constantly receiving the love He has for you that you can then find the ongoing motivation and energy from within to give to the other that personal, unconditional and beneficial love so perfectly demonstrated by our Lord and Savior, Jesus Christ. May you purpose and resolve to learn *from* Him and live *for* Him. This kind of love is the glue that holds marriages together and fills them with a heavenly fragrance so others may see and desire the same reality.

# On Marriage

### HUSBANDS

"Love your wife as Christ loved the church."

Make that your life ambition.

### WIVES

"Submit to your husband – Honor him."

Make it your life ambition to be a wife of noble character whose husband safely trusts, who does him good all the days of his life, and whose husband praises and rises and calls her blessed.

## Secrets of A Happy Marriage

### Divorce Is Not An Option

Never think for a second that divorce is a solution for any problem.

### Let Trials Bring You Together, Not Tear You Apart

Let hard times draw you closer together and to the Lord. Comfort one another and be patient.

### Don't Let The Sun Go Down On Your Wrath

Be open and honest with each other when you disagree. Be careful not to attack the other person's character, only his action.

### Keep Growing In the Lord and In Your Love for Each Other

After over fifty years, you may love each other as much as we do.

God said, "It is not good for man to be alone. I will make a helper suitable for him.

A man shall cleave to his wife and they shall become one flesh." (Genesis 2:24)

# On Being A Wife

### Love Your Husband In Word and Deed

Shower him with praise

Be a submissive wife

Accept your husband, faults and all

Be more concerned about correcting your own faults than his

### Proverbs warns about a nagging wife:

It is better to live on a rooftop than with a nagging wife.

A quarrelsome wife is like constant dripping on a rainy day.

Restraining her is like restraining the wind.

Better to live in a desert than with a quarrelsome and ill-tempered wife.

Better a dry crust with peace and rest than a house full of feasting with strife.

Respect your husband as the head of your home.

Your husband will rise up and call you blessed.

## Before You Become Emotionally Involved
## Learn All You Can About Him

His love for God

His love for his parents

His love for his siblings

# On Building Your Home

### A Wise Woman Builds Her Home With

#### Wisdom

The fear of the Lord is the beginning of WISDOM

God designed families and homes

We must follow His blueprint

Our homes should reflect God's love

#### Understanding

Understanding is studying each family member

Learning what is unique about each one

Being aware of how each one thinks

What are each one's strengths and weaknesses

Seeing how we can encourage and support each one

## Knowledge

Knowing how to make your house a home

Making your home your own original design

Using your personal tastes in decorating your home

Make your home a reflection of you

Then it will be filled with rare and beautiful treasures

*"A foolish woman tears hers down with her own hands."*

Nagging, laziness. selfishness, complaining, discontentment

(Proverbs 12:4; 14:1; 27:15)

# On Being A Mother

Children belong to God

Give them back to God

"Now I give him to the Lord ... for his whole life."

*I Samuel 1:28*


Children are a blessing from God

Thank God for them

"Children are a heritage from the Lord,

a reward from Him."

*Psalm 127:3*

Children Need:

Love

Give them love that comes from God

"God showed His love in that while we were sinners, Christ died for us."

*Romans 5:8*

Encouragement

Give them praise, not criticism

"A gentle answer turns away wrath.

*Proverbs 15:1*

Discipline

Give them boundaries

"A child left to himself brings his mother to shame."

*Proverbs 29:15*

## An Experiment In Positive Expectations

I was teaching kindergarten. It was near the first of the year. I needed to go out of the room for something. When I told the children I had to leave the room, several raised their hands and asked if they could take the names of the children who talked while I was gone. I answered that I did not want to know who talked while I was gone, but that I was interested in the children who did not talk. I told them that I was going to have all the children who were quiet stand up and we would clap for them.

On my return as I approached the room I could hear a little noise, but when I walked in everyone was quiet and in their seats. Hands went up immediately as several wanted to report on the children who had talked. I reminded them that I was not interested in who talked but in who did not talk. I then asked that all who were quiet to stand up. When they did, I led the class in clapping and telling them how proud I was of them.

The next time I left the room I did the same thing. When I returned, all was quiet. We all clapped when everyone stood up. The children learned that good behavior was rewarded.

Such methods helped me to have a wonderful experience teaching kindergarten.

## Philosophy of Discipline
### *Be positive – Be positive – Be positive*

Give your child ten times more positive responses than negative responses.

Always expect the best of your child.

# Mother-in-Law

Loves with Christ's love
Loves her in-laws as her own
Loves freely, unselfishly, unconditionally

"Love covers a multitude of sins."
"A man shall leave his father and mother and cleave unto his wife."

### Naomi – An Example to Follow

Unselfish – put needs of Ruth before herself
Sacrificial – wanted the best for Ruth – a husband
Real – honest about her feelings
Expressed feelings – sadness and happiness
Recognized God's role in her life
Made suggestions – did not interfere
Recognized and appreciated Ruth's love for her

## A World-Class Mother-in-Law

Mother-in-laws are sometimes criticized unmercifully, made fun of, and put down. Many times these attitudes are deserved, but not always. There is a mother-in-law in the Bible who shines bright and clear as a standard for all mothers-in-law to exemplify.

Naomi had two daughters-in-law. Both of them were from godless countries but at some point after they were married, they learned of the true God. Possibly they trusted Him to be their God. As time went on, tragedy struck Naomi's home. She lost her husband and later her two sons. Suddenly Naomi and her two daughters-in-law were left alone with no men to support them. (A widow's life was especially difficult in that time.)

We begin to see Naomi's character. She decided to return to her homeland accompanied by both her daughters-in-law. They must have been a comfort to Naomi. But as the journey was in progress, Naomi began to think of what was best for Orpah and Ruth. They need a husband, she thought: they need to return to their homeland.

Thus the decision was made. When Naomi told Orpah and Ruth, neither of them liked the idea but Orpah reluctantly left. Ruth, however, would not give in. She gave an eloquent summary of her desire: "Where you go, I will go. Your God shall be my God."

One can only surmise that the love Naomi showed to these girls caused Ruth to want to go with Naomi. As they arrived home, Naomi allowed Ruth to make her own decisions about her work. Naomi encouraged her as she worked in the barley fields.

A key quality that Naomi possessed was her unselfishness. She must have enjoyed having Ruth live with her, but she knew that it would be better for Ruth to have a husband and her own home. Naomi encouraged and helped Ruth to meet this need. Naomi left a legacy for all mothers-in-law to follow. Love, respect, unselfishness, and putting others before yourself will make you a mother-in-law to be praised and honored.

# Being A Great Daughter-in-Law

## Respect Your Mother-in-Law

## Learn From Your Mother-in-Law

### Things Ruth Learned From Naomi

She learned about God—
enough to want to know God for herself

She learned how to handle change

She learned how to handle sorrow

She learned how to admit when she was wrong

She learned acceptance

She learned how to be an obedient wife

RECOGNIZE THAT YOU CAN LEARN FROM
YOUR MOTHER-IN-LAW

BE WILLING TO ASK FOR AND TAKE ADVICE

BE WILLING TO ADMIT WHEN YOU ARE WRONG

# On Being A Grandmother

A grandmother has the chance to do a better job the second time around.

A grandmother can just enjoy her grandchildren without the responsibility for them.

A grandmother can be the link to the past for her grandchildren.

Relate to them your faith, your walk with God, how God has led you.

G —— godly example

R —— ready to listen

A —— always attentive

N —— never too busy

D —— does fun things

M —— makes memories

O —— open heart and home

T —— true to word

H —— heart for God

E —— easy to talk to

R —— relays the truth

*Dedicated to my grandchildren:*
*Beth Ann, Ashley, Joshua, David, Alison*
*with whom I spent treasured moments*
*and made wonderful memories*

## Memory Making With My Grandchildren

After I became a grandmother, I began to wonder how I would get to know our grandchildren. I felt very strongly that the only way to really get to know them was to be with them without their parents.

The solution turned out to be COUSINS CAMP. Each summer during their elementary-age years, we had camp with the five grandchildren. Each day was filled with fun activities, helping with the kitchen chores, crafts, Bible time, and special events. As they got older, the activities changed as we tried to keep up with their new maturity and interests. One summer the boys ruled out crafts. Short trips began. One very special trip that everyone loved was to Atlanta to watch the Atlanta Braves play baseball. Our last COUSINS CAMP was a trip to New York City. What fun we had seeing all the sights, having a hot dog from the vendor at the street corner. That trip sadly was our last official COUSINS CAMP. But all five of the children love to be together. We make every effort to make that happen as often as possible. What wonderful memories we have made through the years.

# Valentine's Day

A time to open our hearts to those we love

A time to share words of encouragement

### Qualities That I See In You

V – VALUE

A – APPPRECIATION

L – LOVE

E – ENCOURAGEMENT

N – NURTURING

T – TRUST

I – INVOLVEMENT

N – NOBLENESS

E – ESTEEMING

## Love From I Corinthians 13

*Love is patient, kind*

*Love is not proud, rude, self seeking*

*Love does not boast, is not subject to evil*

*Love keeps no record of wrongs*

*Love rejoices in the truth*

*Love always trusts, protects, hopes, perseveres*

## Thoughts About Love

Love is not shallow – love deeply

Love is not selfish – love widely

Love is not possessive – love freely

Love is not perfect – love forgivingly

Thank you for loving me, accepting me,
and, most of all, for being my friend.

## Roses Say "I Love You"

I was so groggy after the gall bladder surgery and still had a tube down my throat. They wheeled me back into my room after my time in recovery and placed my bed next to the night stand which was in front of the window. I half-opened my eyes and glanced toward the window. There seemed to be something red and tall on the nightstand. I struggled to open my eyes wider. When I did, I saw a vase of long-stem red roses in all their glory seemingly looking down on me and saying "I love you." When I was more alert and awake, I found out that they were from some dear friends. I had never before received such a beautiful gift of flowers. To this day when I think of roses, I think of those dear friends.

My husband observed how much I appreciated the roses. Some years later, I happened to be out of town visiting my parents on our wedding anniversary. There came a knock at the door. A florist delivered twenty long stem red roses! Even though we were apart, I felt his love keenly as I looked lovingly at the beautiful roses.

When I was younger, I used to think that flowers were such a waste of money. They were good for nothing but to look at, smell, and, if you have allergies, sneeze at. I don't think that way anymore as I see flowers as the perfect way to say "I love you." You spend a lot of money for something that doesn't last and is not at all practical. But to the person who receives the flowers, it shows that you care enough to spend your money for something that does nothing but show them the depth of your love. It is like Mary in the Bible who poured expensive perfume on Jesus' feet and was criticized for such a waste of money. But Jesus seemed to approve. I have to feel that He approves of our pouring out our love for others in a tangible way.

I get roses almost every year now for some occasion, and they always say to me, as nothing else can, "You are greatly loved."

# Clutter vs Organization

CLUTTER IS ONE PERSON'S TRASH,
ANOTHER PERSON'S TREASURE

ORGANIZED CLUTTER VERSUS DISORGANIZED CLUTTER

Organized – things you want to keep because of
sentimental reasons or their value

Disorganized – things you have put aside because you
don't want to deal with them
or you can't make a decision about them

CLUTTER REPRESENTS THE PAST –
TRYING TO HOLD ON TO THE PAST

CLUTTER REPRESENTS AN UNORGANIZED LIFE

Be organized – find a place for everything and keep
everything in its place

Keep important things and those used
most often easily accessible

Closets and drawers should be organized
with like things together

Use file cabinets for important papers;
keep current papers in front

Get rid of unnecessary items

Use plastic storage boxes for storing seasonal items:
Label them – Keep in attic or basement

*I Corinthians 14:33*
*"For God is not a God of disorder but of peace."*

## Clutter Grows

Our first home was a church parsonage that was shaped like a square box divided into four rooms with the bathroom and closets in the middle. The kitchen had a table in the middle of the room with barely enough space to put four chairs around it. Our two sons were born while we lived there. Needless to say we had no room for clutter. I found that if even one or two things were out of place, the whole house looked messy. I also found that if there were dirty dishes in the kitchen, the room looked messy.

I learned a valuable lesson about how clutter grows one Thanksgiving. My sister had flown down for the holidays, and I had prepared the traditional dinner and in the process had made a huge mess. Right after we finished dinner we headed for the airport. As soon as we got home from the airport, my husband had to leave for a pastor's meeting. It was evening and I was left with two fussy sons and a horribly messy kitchen. I kept looking at the kitchen but continued to procrastinate until it was time for bed. I rationalized that I would be more ready to tackle it in the morning. Wrong! In the daylight it seemed to be ten times worse than the night before. I finally got the kitchen cleaned but with great effort. I vowed that I would never let things get so out of control again.

A good lesson to learn, especially when it involves dirty dishes and clutter, is that it can multiply before we realize it.

# Listen To the Animals

## Proverbs 30:25-28 Four Small Animals

### Ant

very small

weak

works tirelessly

works together

wise

stores food for winter

### Coney

humble

little power

accepts weaknesses

makes home in rocks

knows protection is from God

### Locust

orderly

organized

have no king

cooperate

### Lizard

weak, puny

found in palaces

can be caught with hand

fearless

not afraid to go anywhere

### Psalm 42:1-2 Like the Deer

Pants for water – we pant, desire greatly, God's Word

### Isaiah 40:31 Like the Eagle

run and not grow weary

walk and not faint

our strength comes from God

Matthew 5:20-23 Like the Birds of the Air
God knows when each bird falls to the ground—
God provides what each bird needs

## Wisdom of Birds

(excerpt from a poem by an unknown author)

Said the robin to the sparrow, "Friend, I wonder why it is that these anxious human beings rush about and worry so." Said the sparrow to the robin, "Friend I think that it must be that they have no Heavenly Father such as cares for you and me."

## Listen To The Animals

Jerry and I were in Chicago with our senior citizens where we visited the Chicago Aquarium. One of the most interesting exhibits was the dolphin show. The first part of the program was a demonstration of the ways the dolphins are trained. As I listened, I could not believe what I was hearing. It sounded as though the trainer was talking about children.

The first thing they teach dolphins is to trust their trainer. Nothing else can be taught until the dolphin learns to trust his master. How remarkable! The first thing we must teach our children is that they can trust us and most of all that they can trust God. And how is that accomplished? We must do the things we need to do to earn their trust and be so very careful not to do anything that would cause them to lose their trust in us. We earn their trust by keeping our word – not promising things and then not keeping that promise. We earn their trust by showing them that we care about them, that we believe in them, and that we always think the best of them.

The next thing I observed about the dolphin was that their trainers always expect good behavior from them and are very careful to acknowledge their good behavior and to reward it. In conjunction with expecting good behavior, the trainers are always consistent. They do things the same way every time so the dolphin knows what to expect and therefore lives up to that expectation.

The last thing I observed was that the trainers had a goal for the dolphin to accomplish and continually worked the dolphin to strive to attain the goal. With our children we must discover what they are capable of accomplishing and then encourage them to reach the mark. Be their greatest fan and their most loyal cheerleader. They won't disappoint you!

Listen and Learn FROM THE ANIMALS!

# On Growing Older

STAY FRESH AND GREEN
Be open to new ideas
Keep learning and trying new things
Be willing to change
"Do not say, "Why were the old days better?""

FLOURISH AS A PALM TREE
Keep growing in the Lord
Keep learning from God's Word
Keep God and others as your focus
"They that wait on the Lord shall renew their strength"

BEAR FRUIT IN OLD AGE

Have God's perspective

Never stop serving the Lord

Spend your time and money on things that count for eternity

"Whose leaf does not wither —

whatever they do prospers."

*(Psalm 92; Ecclesiastes 7:10; Isaiah 40:31; Psalm 1:3b NIV)*

## My Grandmother

Lee Ann Curtis

May 1877- February 1967

### GROWING OLD WITH HONOR AND DIGNITY

I have wonderful memories of my Granny, as we called her. She was a very educated, self-motivated, caring person. I found out in later years that she was a college graduate. How remarkable! We lived two blocks from her so I spent a lot of time at her house. She was a very devoted wife. She had dinner on the table right when my granddad came home from work every day.

She lived by a schedule which enabled her to always be on top of things. Her house was always clean, neat, and organized. She went to her church activities every week. She entertained her family at all the holidays and cooked everything herself.

The thing that impressed me most about her was that she believed in me and encouraged me. She was positive and affirming to me. Once I overheard her tell my aunt that I wanted to go to Wheaton College which was a thousand miles away from home and very expensive. But she said that when I wanted to do something I usually did it and that she was sure that would be the case. Another time I remember very vividly was at Thanksgiving. I had asked her if I could help in the kitchen. She gave me the whipping cream to whip. She warned me not to whip it too long. But somehow I did and before I knew it the cream was practically butter. But when I told her what had happened she didn't get mad at me but gave me some money to go to the store and buy more. Then she reminded me again not to whip it too much. Believe me, I didn't. Her faith in me helped me to accomplish goals in my life that I might not have been able to otherwise.

As Granny grew older she retained her sharp mind, keen wit, and knowledge of the news. We could discuss almost any current event and be knowledgeable about it. She was ninety when she died. I am so thankful to the Lord for her. What a legacy she left for me!

## Finishing Well

"I have fought the good fight, I have kept the faith"

### THE CHRISTIAN LIFE IS A MARATHON NOT A SPRINT

It is not so important how we begin—How we end is what counts

### EXAMPLES OF THOSE WHO FINISHED WELL

PAUL – II Timothy 4:7

"I have finished my course, I have kept the faith. Now there is in store for me the crown of righteousness…"

### MOSES – DEUTERONOMY 34:8-12

Moses was 120 years old when he died, His eyes were not weak nor his strength gone. The Lord knew Moses face to face. No one has ever shown the mighty power that Moses did.

## JOSHUA – Joshua 24:28-31

Joshua the servant of the Lord died at the age of 110. Israel served the Lord throughout the lifetime of Joshua.

## JEHOSHAPHAT – II Chronicles 20:31-32

Jehoshaphat reigned 25 years. He walked in the ways of his father Asa and did not stray from them. He did what was right in the eyes of the Lord.

## CALEB – Joshua 14:5-14

Caleb followed the Lord whole heartedly. He was 85 years old when he took his mountain and said he was still as strong as he was 45 years before.

### Example of One Who Did Not Finish Well

#### Solomon – I Kings 11:4-6

As Solomon grew older, his wives turned his heart toward other gods. His heart was not fully devoted to the Lord his God. He did not serve the Lord completely.

# My Grandfather

ROBERT BELLE HEARN

February 26, 1864 - February 8, 1961

BURNING OUT, NOT RUSTING OUT
A Texas rancher who lost everything during
the hard economic times
Moved to Ft. Worth, Texas, and opened a
grocery store with my father.
The depression hit soon after and they lost everything.
Had no retirement like Social Security so was forced to
live with his children
all of whom were struggling to survive.
During the time he lived with us he walked up and down
the streets selling Raleigh products.
When he was ninety, he memorized many verses from the Bible
and listed over 260 verses he had learned.

These are some of his last words:

*May these verses brighten your way*

*And guide and comfort your day*

*Just as I've gotten hope and joy*

*To struggle on, to trust, and to pray*

*for courage to be*

*"A MAN ONCE AND NOT TWICE A BOY"*

*Ready to go and ready, my Lord,*

*Should You come today*

*Learn them*

*Trust in their messages*

*Live in their holy precepts.*

Your devoted, doting, old granddad